AF131348

BOOK ANALYSIS

By Isabelle Bousquette

The Beautiful and Damned

BY F. SCOTT FITZGERALD

F. SCOTT FITZGERALD

AMERICAN NOVELIST AND SHORT STORY WRITER

- **Born in St. Paul, Minnesota in 1896.**
- **Died in Hollywood, California in 1940.**
- **Notable works:**
  - *This Side of Paradise* (1920), novel
  - *The Great Gatsby* (1925), novel
  - *Tender is the Night* (1934), novel

Francis Scott Fitzgerald was an American writer most famous for his touching and often tragic depictions of the Jazz Age. After attending a boys' school in Minnesota, Fitzgerald found his way to Princeton, where he became occupied with attaining social status. He spent time writing about the spirit of America, interested in both its romance and its vulgarity. Ultimately, Fitzgerald left Princeton to fight in the First World War.

In 1920, Fitzgerald published *This Side of Paradise*, a semi-autobiographical novel that made him famous on the literary scene. Fitzgerald moved with his family to France, joining a group of American literary and artistic expatriates that had become disillusioned with their country. This group, which included Ernest Hemingway (American novelist, 1899-1961) and Gertrude Stein (American novelist, 1974-1946), became known as the Lost Generation. In 1925, Fitzgerald published his most famous novel, *The Great Gatsby*, which stood as a testament to the futility of the American dream.

THE BEAUTIFUL AND DAMNED

A JAZZ-AGE TRAGEDY

- **Genre:** novel
- **Reference edition:** Fitzgerald, F. S. (2010) *The Beautiful and Damned*. London: Random House.
- **1st edition:** 1922
- **Themes:** marriage, money, high society, alcohol, prohibition, the Jazz Age, the Lost Generation

The Beautiful and Damned was published in 1922, two years after Fitzgerald's debut novel, *This Side of Paradise*. While *This Side of Paradise* followed a young man through his youth and adolescence, *The Beautiful and Damned* follows a young couple through their courtship, marriage and ultimate marital struggles. The novel centres around Anthony Patch and Gloria Gilbert, two young and beautiful New York socialites. His grandfather is a famous millionaire. She has a certain charm that has men constantly fawning over her.

However, a mix of entitlement, laziness and extravagant expenditures quickly land the couple with severe money problems. Unwilling to give up their luxurious lifestyle, their problems get even worse when Anthony's grandfather decides to disinherit him.

Anthony and Gloria become icons of a Lost Generation. They throw parties, drink and spend money constantly but fail to find any true purpose in life. They become an antithesis to the American Dream, the idea that a better life awaits those who work hard. In fact, they often stumble across employment opportunities, but find no motivation to work hard or indeed to work at all. The American Dream is, for Fitzgerald, dead. Instead, it is replaced with an age of luxury and parties: the Jazz Age.

Anthony and Gloria are characters who uncover the dark side of the Jazz Age. We see them face the harsh consequences of endless parties, drinking and disregard for the prohibition laws. Their lives ultimately tread the direction of one long cosmic hangover. Some have read the characters as inspired by Fitzgerald and his wife, Zelda, who partook in a similar social scene. However, the novel is more often read as a manifestation of Fitzgerald and Zelda's fears about their lifestyle than a reflection of their actual struggles.

SUMMARY

COURTSHIP AND MARRIAGE

The novel opens with a description of Anthony Patch's early life. Both his mother and father passed away when he was young, so he was entrusted to his grandfather, Adam Patch. Adam Patch had been a famous Civil War hero, a Wall Street millionaire and, later in his life, a prohibition activist. He would like to see his grandson do something with his life. Anthony attends Harvard and then travels around Europe. He tells his grandfather that he may write histories, but soon tires of the idea. He moves to an apartment in New York, where he lives off money provided yearly by his grandfather.

In New York, Anthony spends his nights with his friends Dick Caramel and Maury Noble. One day, Dick introduces Anthony to his cousin, Gloria Gilbert. Anthony and Gloria are immediately attracted to each other and begin seeing more and more of each other. However, the first time Anthony kisses Gloria, she becomes uncomfortable and asks to leave. She is being courted by other men, most notably her father's friend, Joseph Bloeckman.

Anthony soon realises that he is in love with Gloria and continues to pursue her. She is coy at first but soon agrees that they should marry. They dream of spending their lives together, but more than anything, about the inheritance they will one day receive from Anthony's grandfather.

AFTER THE HONEYMOON

After Anthony and Gloria marry, they begin fighting about many little things. He becomes frustrated about her specific dietary desires and she begins to believe he is a coward. The two also bicker about who will send out the laundry. At one point, their disagreements become somewhat physical on a train platform in Redgate. The incident is forgiven, but it alters the core of their relationship. Ultimately, they decide to settle down in a grey house in Marietta.

Anthony and Gloria consider different ways to spend their time. Anthony thinks he might become a war correspondent or enter the bond business (both at the behest of his grandfather). Neither of these considerations last long. Gloria considers going into the movies and even becoming pregnant. Again, neither of these plans materialise. The couple ends up spending the majority of their time throwing parties. As their house comes to feel more like a prison, the couple turn to alcohol. At one particularly raucous party, Anthony's grandfather coincidentally drops in. As a staunch prohibitionist, he is less than impressed and promptly departs. Anthony and Gloria immediately become concerned about their inheritance.

Anthony tries to make amends with his grandfather, but Adam Patch refuses to see him. He passes away soon after and leaves Anthony nothing in his will. Anthony and Gloria, now cognisant of their financial problems, move into a small apartment in the city. They commence a lawsuit to contest Adam Patch's will.

THE WAR

When America declares war against Germany, Anthony, Dick and Maury enlist in the officers' corps. Anthony is rejected due to his blood pressure; however, he is soon conscripted into the army and no mention is thence made of his blood pressure. While Gloria stays in New York, Anthony goes into training at Camp Hooker. As their letters become less frequent, Anthony strikes up an affair with a young woman named Dot. When Anthony's regiment announces a move to Mississippi, Dot threatens to kill herself if Anthony leaves her. Anthony agrees to pay for her to stay in a boarding house near him in Mississippi.

Dot calls Anthony out of the blue and again implies that she is going to kill herself. Anthony sneaks out of camp to see her and then faces disciplinary actions. Gloria, still in New York, has also had the opportunity for affairs, but has decided to remain, on the whole, faithful to her husband. This is more due to a lack of attractive prospects than to any real devotion. The announcement of the end of the war coincides with the announcement that their lawsuit against Adam Patch will soon be decided. Anthony then returns to New York, never having been deployed abroad.

DESPERATE TIMES

While Anthony and Gloria eagerly await the decision of the lawsuit, their financial situation becomes increasingly dire. Anthony briefly gets a job in sales, but soon gives up when he realises that he cannot sell anything. Gloria reaches out to Joseph Bloeckman and asks him to put her in the movies. After an awkward screen test, she is told that she is too old for the particular role. Humiliated, she gives up on the idea.

Anthony and Gloria spend most of their time drinking. Anthony becomes a regular at speakeasies and the two lose touch with most of their former friends. This becomes starkly evident when they realise that they have no one to ask for money. The day the lawsuit is set to be announced, Dot appears on Anthony's doorstep begging to resume their relationship. When she refuses to leave, Anthony gets angry and raises a chair to hit her. We are not told exactly how the incident resolves itself because Anthony blacks out, but the last thing he hears is a snapping sound. Gloria arrives home to find Anthony obsessing over his stamp collection. She tells him that they won the lawsuit and have inherited 30 million dollars.

The last scene takes place on a cruise ship. Other passengers gossip about the infamy of Anthony and Gloria. They say that he has gone mad because his grandfather's confidant, Shuttleworth, committed suicide after Anthony's winning lawsuit. However, Anthony is actually satisfied with himself and believes that he has triumphed in the face of adversity to ultimately come out on top.

CHARACTER STUDY

ANTHONY PATCH

Anthony is the protagonist of the work, but he is far from being its hero. He is considered clean and handsome. Fitzgerald describes his physical appearance, saying:

> "He was secretly orderly and in person spick and span—his friends declared that they had never seen his hair rumpled. His nose was too sharp; his mouth was one of those unfortunate mirrors of mood inclined to droop perceptibly in moments of unhappiness, but his blue eyes were charming, whether alert with intelligence or half closed in an expression of melancholy humor" (pp. 16-17)

He begins the novel as a sympathetic character. We discover that both of his parents have passed away and he has found refuge in his stamp collection and the self-assured confidence that comes with being the grandson of the renowned Adam J. Patch.

However, what begins as confidence quickly grows into a sense of entitlement. He has no motivation to work hard or prove himself. When he falls in love with Gloria Gilbert, his whole being becomes consumed with winning her. Once he does that, his life again becomes purposeless.

As the novel goes on, the charming socialite grandson of Adam J. Patch betrays some deeply dark moments. He strikes his wife on a train platform. When he and Gloria fall on hard times, he uses their money to pay for lodgings for his mistress, Dot. Finally, the most startling moment of the novel is when he throws an oak chair at Dot.

Does he kill her? There is no mention of a body when Gloria returns to the house. Fitzgerald writes: "with almost a tangible snapping sound the face of the world changed before his eyes…" (p. 390), hinting that her neck was indeed snapped. Or was Dot's appearance on his doorstep simply a symptom of his alcohol-induced madness? Regardless of whether Anthony is a madman or a murderer, he is undoubtedly a very sick man and a quintessential antihero.

GLORIA GILBERT

Gloria is introduced into the story as the cousin of Anthony's friend, Dick Caramel. She is a beautiful and wild young socialite. However, there is something special about her, a certain charm that constantly attracts male attention. Maury Noble remarks that she has "the outer signs of the cut-and-dried Yale prom girl and all that—but different, very emphatically different" (p. 50).

If Anthony derives an inherent yet unearned sense of self-worth from his famous grandfather, Gloria derives that same unearned sense of self-worth from her beauty. In a brief poetic aside in the work, Fitzgerald describes the goddess beauty coming down to inhabit a body on earth; we are to imagine that that true essence of beauty has found its home in Gloria. Fitzgerald tells us: "She was dazzling—alight; it was agony to comprehend her beauty in a glance. Her hair, full of a heavenly glamour, was gay against the winter color of the room" (p. 57).

Gloria and Anthony build their identities around being young, rich and beautiful. However, as the novel continues, they become older, poorer and less attractive. Gloria decides that she does not want children because she thinks that doing so would make her less beautiful. As each birthday passes, she worries about losing her beauty. When Gloria auditions for the movies and is told that she is too old for the role, she realises that her beauty has faded, and she has lost the one thing that made her feel superior.

DICK CARAMEL

In many ways, Dick Caramel represents the man Anthony could have been. Anthony continually scoffs at Dick for his tendency to "trot home and work on his book" (p. 24). Fitzgerald describes him, saying: "He has yellowish eyes—one of them startlingly clear, the other opaque as a muddy pool—and a bulging brow like a funny-paper baby" (p. 27). In the beginning of the story, he is the butt of several of Anthony and Maury's jokes.

However, Caramel is a foil for Anthony in the sense that he has the one thing Anthony lacks: motivation to succeed. He enters the world intending "to accomplish a vague yearnful something which would react either in eternal reward or, at the least, in the personal satisfaction of having striven for the greatest good of the greatest number" (p. 71). While Anthony spends his days at Harvard being reclusive and collecting stamps, Caramel decides to become a writer and becomes the editor of the Harvard Crimson.

Ultimately, Caramel's novel, *The Demon Lover*, is a huge success. Its success makes both Anthony and Gloria uncomfortable, giving them a sense that the world is moving on whilst they are accomplishing nothing. In order to reassert her superiority, Gloria expounds that she has not read *The Demon Lover*. As Caramel continues writing successfully, Gloria and Anthony fall upon financial strife. When they ultimately turn to Caramel for help, he responds with contempt, having remembered Gloria's comment seven years later.

ANALYSIS

THE TRAGIC GENRE

In many ways, *The Beautiful and Damned* is a novel which follows the same tropes as dramatic tragedy. The central tenet of tragedy is that its characters slowly spiral towards a devastating fate due to a fatal flaw with themselves. That is certainly the case here. Still, at times, Fitzgerald even goes as far as to veer out of the novel genre and into drama. He introduces Anthony at the beginning as "the hero" (p. 14). As stated above, throughout the story, Anthony is far more anti-hero than hero material. However, Fitzgerald's use of the world "hero" clearly conjures connotations of the dramatic tragic hero.

Occasionally, the dialogue within the book is even presented in the form of a dramatic script. This is most striking in the chapter entitled "A Flash-back in Paradise" (p. 32). At this point, Fitzgerald introduces the character of the goddess of beauty and explains how she comes to earth. The insertion of a pagan deity is jarring and occurs nowhere else in the novel. However, its inclusion creates an atmosphere not unlike that of a Greek tragedy, in which gods and goddesses often acted as characters and affected the lives of mortals.

The goddess of beauty and the dramatic dialogue thus often imbue the novel with an air of tragic performance. As such, painting Anthony and Gloria as characters in a generic tragedy secures their fate and the narrative direction of the story. Just like in dramatic tragedies, Anthony and Gloria fall due to their own misdoings, or "tragic flaws". Fitzgerald here is clearly drawing on traditional tragic tropes and seems to be influenced to a certain extent by Greek drama.

MARRIAGE

This novel is one is which marriage is truly put to the test. Anthony and Gloria are wildly passionate about each other before their marriage. However, the act of their marriage is presented in the novel somewhat oddly and without incident. From Anthony's perspective, Fitzgerald writes: "A languorous and pleasant content settled like a weight upon him bringing responsibility and possession. He was married" (p. 141). From Gloria's perspective it is presented with: "in a moment she would be forever and securely safe" (*ibid.*). They are a couple who believe themselves to be extraordinary and superior. However, marriage becomes for them the same thing it is for all other couples: a societal custom that leads to security and one which Anthony declared he would never enter, previously stating "I am entirely opposed to marriage for people of my type" (p. 87).

Fitzgerald uses the institution of marriage in the novel to exemplify a larger disillusionment with life. Towards the end of the novel, Anthony says to his mistress, Dot: "once I wanted something and got it. It was the only thing I ever wanted badly, Dot. And when I got it it turned to dust in my hands" (p. 299). He is, of course, referring to Gloria and his marriage to her. Throughout the novel we constantly get the sense that something is fading, whether it be desire, passion, purpose or romance. By the end, his encounters with Gloria, which had once been "the most stimulating", become benign, "without conflict, without fear, without elation" (p. 191). Winning Gloria had been the only thing for which Anthony actually strived in his life. Without that pressure to win her, he again feels useless and impotent.

ALCOHOLISM, PROHIBITION AND THE JAZZ AGE

Prohibition plays an important role in the background of this novel. Although the technicalities of it are never discussed, contemporary readers would have understood that prohibition, or the act of making the manufacturing, sale and transportation of alcohol illegal, came into effect within the timeline of the novel.

We know that Adam J. Patch is a strict moralist and avid prohibitionist. Thus, when he walks in on Anthony and Gloria's alcohol-filled soiree in Marietta, the scene is all the more awkward and disturbing. Fitzgerald heightens the drama by telling us that "Not one is aware that Adam Patch has that morning made a contribution of fifty thousand dollars to the cause of national prohibition" (p. 243). Thus, Anthony's general laziness and dependence on his grandfather's money is painted as even more terrible when we see the way he disrespects the elder Patch.

During the Jazz Age, the prohibition of alcohol makes it all the more romanticised. Fitzgerald explains why Anthony relies more and more on drinking:

> "When prohibition came in July he found that, among those who could afford it, there was more drinking than ever before. One's host now brought out a bottle upon the slightest pretext. The tendency to display liquor was a manifestation of the same instinct that led a man to deck his wife with jewels. To have liquor was a boast, almost a badge of respectability." (p. 340)

Thus, for Anthony, alcohol becomes not only a way to avoid his problems, but a way to prove that he does not have any. In a moment when his money is running out, the consumption of alcohol, he believes, proves that his money problems are temporary and insignificant. Alcohol becomes the key tenet of his lifestyle because it becomes proof for him that his lifestyle is respectable. He continually justifies significant over-drinking, ultimately becoming an alcoholic.

The Jazz Age stands as a lavish historical moment of extravagant parties. However, here Fitzgerald showcases its dark underbelly. Anthony wastes his last dollar at a speakeasy and is too drunk to get home. A man on the street tries to help him, but ultimately gets angry when he realises Anthony cannot even repay him for the cab. We can see here how distinctly gross and un-romantic alcohol becomes in excess. It is clear that alcoholism contributes to Anthony and Gloria's financial problems and the problems in their marriage. What is less clear is the degree to which it drives Anthony to ultimate madness and the role it plays in his final encounter with Dot. Nevertheless, in a world where prohibition created an exciting age of parties, we see the distinct dangers of excess.

THE LOST GENERATION AND THE END OF THE AMERICAN DREAM

Fitzgerald belonged to a literary movement called "the Lost Generation", in which a group of American writers lost faith in the American Dream. Writers such as Fitzgerald, along with Ernest Hemingway, John Dos Passos (American novelist, 1896-1970), E.E. Cummings (American poet, 1894-1962), Archibald MacLeish (American poet, 1892-1982), Hart Crane (American poet, 1899-1932) and others, moved to Paris to conti-nue writing about the loss of American ideals.

The protagonists in many of their works fought in World War I only to return to an America that had lost both its charm and its meaning for them.

The lack of purpose and ennui characteristic of this generation can easily be seen in the characters of Anthony and Gloria. The previous generation had been built upon, motivated by and inspired by the fantasy of the American Dream. In many ways, the character of Adam J. Patch embodies that dream: a man who worked hard and raised himself up in the world. However, Anthony and Gloria fail to see the point in completing any kind of work.

Anthony briefly considers working for an entrepreneur named Sammy Carleton. For Sammy, the American Dream is alive and he compares himself to magnates such as John D. Rockefeller (American industrialist, 1839-1937). He offers to employ Anthony selling copies of his inspirational book, "Heart Talks." However, just as Anthony mocked Dick Caramel for working on his book, he relates the business of Sammy "with an accompaniment of ironic laughter" (p. 334). After being pushed by Gloria, Anthony actually tries to sell some of the books, finds it rather difficult, and ends up frequenting bars instead. The American Dream no longer carries, for him, the promise of a greater future. He instead chooses to wait for the lawsuit contesting his grandfather's will. He does not see the point in truly trying to accomplish anything and begins to view life, as well as all the endeavours within it, as pointless.

In the last line of the book, after winning the lawsuit against Adam Patch's will, Anthony thinks: "I showed them...it was a hard fight, but I didn't give up and I came through!" (p. 393). These lines can easily be read as an ironic mockery of the American Dream. Anthony believes that he has worked hard and persevered to come out on top. In fact, he did the exact opposite. Persevering for him meant doing absolutely nothing. Thus, the American Dream is lost and replaced by a world where prosperity is random and hard work is often fruitless.

FURTHER REFLECTION

SOME QUESTIONS TO THINK ABOUT...

- Do you believe that Anthony, having inherited his grandfather's 30 million dollars, ultimately comes out on top? Explain your answer.
- Does Fitzgerald romanticise or criticise the Jazz Age? Or both? Explain your answer.
- How does the relationship between Anthony and Gloria develop over the course of the novel?
- Why do you believe Anthony and Gloria never follow through on any of the opportunities that come their way?
- Why do Anthony and Gloria party so excessively? Do you think the reason changes over the course of the novel?
- Why does Anthony decide to cheat on Gloria? Why does Gloria decide not to cheat on Anthony? How do these decisions affect their relationship?

- What do you think actually happens in Anthony's final encounter with Dot? An assault? A murder? Or was it all simply imagined by a maddened alcoholic brain?
- Are there any characters in the novel we are meant to emulate? Or is this simply a cautionary tale? Explain your answer.
- How does the novel reflect Fitzgerald's fears about his own life and the society in which he lived?

We want to hear from you!
Leave a comment on your online library
and share your favourite books on social media!

FURTHER READING

REFERENCE EDITION

- Fitzgerald, F. S. (2010) *The Beautiful and Damned.* London: Random House.

REFERENCE STUDIES

- Mizener, A. (2018) F. Scott Fitzgerald: American Writer. *Encyclopædia Britannica.* [Online]. [Accessed 27 December 2018]. Available from: <https://www.britannica.com/biography/F-Scott-Fitzgerald>

- The Editors of Encyclopædia Britannica (2017) Lost Generation: American Literature. *Encyclopædia Britannica.* [Online]. [Accessed 27 December 2018]. Available from: <https://www.britannica.com/topic/Lost-Generation>

- The Editors of Encyclopædia Britannica (2018) Prohibition: United States History, 1920-1933. *Encyclopædia Britannica.* [Online]. [Accessed 19 January 2019]. Available from: <https://www.britannica.com/event/Prohibition-United-States-history-1920-1933>

ADDITIONAL SOURCES

- Bruccoli, M. (1981) *Some Sort of Epic Grandeur: The Life of F. Scott Fitzgerald.* Columbia: University of South Carolina Press.

- Bruccoli, M. and Baughman, J. S. (2004) *Conversations with F. Scott Fitzgerald.* Jackson: University Press of Mississippi.

- Curnutt, K. (2004) *A Historical Guide to F. Scott Fitzgerald.* New York: Oxford University Press.

- Mizener, A. (1951) *The Far Side of Paradise.* Boston: Houghton Mifflin.

- Prigozy, R. (2002) *The Cambridge Companion to F. Scott Fitzgerald.* Cambridge: Cambridge University Press.

ADAPTATIONS

- *The Beautiful and Damned.* (1922) [Film]. William A. Seiter. Dir. USA: Warner Bros.

- *The Beautiful and Damned.* (2010) [Film]. Richard Wolstencroft. Dir. Australia: Accent Film Entertainment.

MORE FROM BRIGHTSUMMARIES.COM

- Reading guide – *The Great Gatsby* by F. Scott Fitzgerald.

- Reading guide – *This Side of Paradise* by F. Scott Fitzgerald.

www.brightsummaries.com

Ebook EAN: 9782808017183

Paperback EAN: 9782808017190

Legal Deposit: D/2019/12603/26

Cover: © Primento

Digital conception by Primento, the digital partner of publishers.